Jewish Songs old & new

ADON OLAM

Traditional

3

AYN KAYLOKAYNU

Traditional

Allegro Moderato

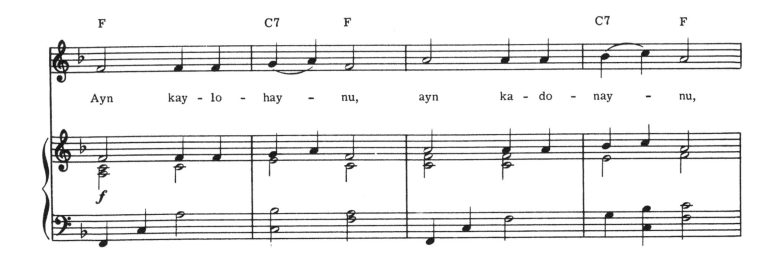

Ayn kay-lo-hay - nu, ayn ka-do-nay - nu,

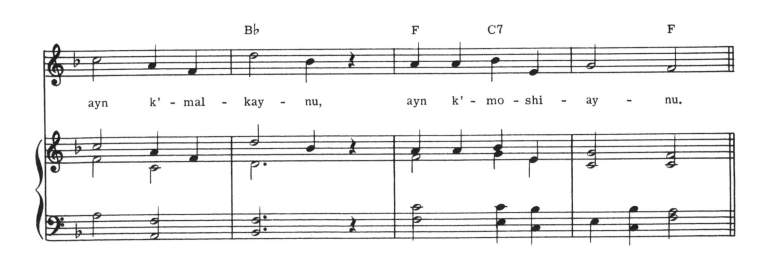

ayn k'-mal-kay-nu, ayn k'-mo-shi-ay - nu.

5

ADIR HU

Traditional

A - dir hu, a - dir hu, yiv - ne vay - to b' - ka rov,

bim' - he - ra,_____ bim' - he - ra, b'ya - may - nu b' - ka - rov.

El b' - ne, ayl b' - ne, b'ne vayt - cha b' - ka - rov.

ELI, ELI

Traditional

8

THE EXODUS SONG

Words by PAT BOONE
Music by ERNEST GOLD

HALLELUJA

Words and Music by
K. OSHRAT and S. ORR

HATIKVA

Words and Music by
HESKEL BRISMAN

Maestoso

Kol od _____ ba - le - vav p'ni - ma

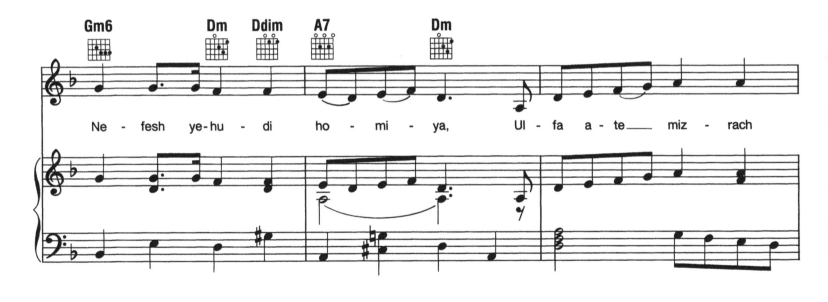

Ne - fesh ye - hu - di ho - mi - ya, Ul - fa - a - te ___ miz - rach

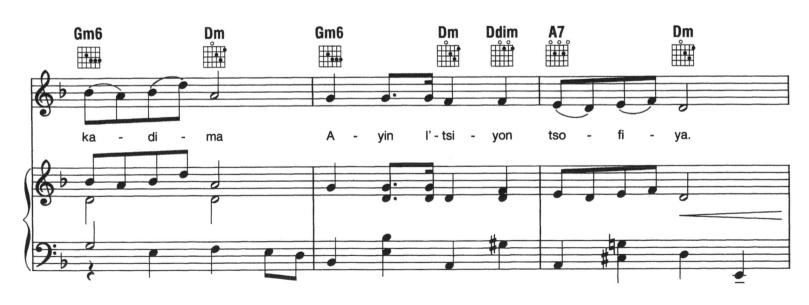

ka - di - ma A - yin l' - tsi - yon tso - fi - ya.

8 bassa

HAVAH NAGILAH

Traditional
Adaptation by NEIL DIAMOND

Start slowly and accelerate to end

Ha - vah nagi - lah, Ha - vah nagi - lah,

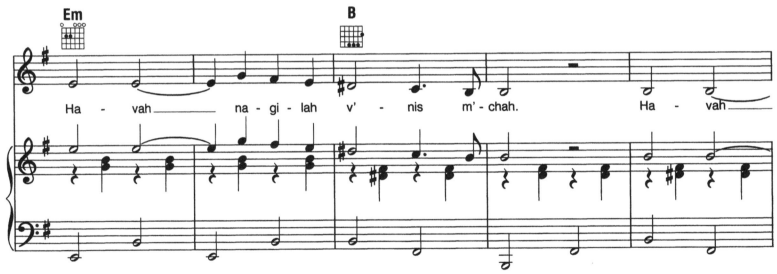

Ha - vah nagi - lah v' - nis m' - chah. Ha - vah

na - gi - lah, Ha - vah nagi - lah, Ha - vah

KOL-NIDRE

Traditional

HINAY MA TOV

Traditional

IF I WERE A RICH MAN

(From the Musical "FIDDLER ON THE ROOF")

Words by SHELDON HARNICK
Music by JERRY BOCK

ISRAELI LULLABY

Words and Music by
HESKEL BRISMAN

JERUSALEM, JERUSALEM
(Yerushala'im Shel Zahav)

English Lyrics by NORMAN NEWELL
Original Hebrew Words and Music by NAOMI SHEMER

gold, My heart will sing your songs of glo - ry, Je -

ru - sa - lem. ___ The / And

lem. ___

rall. e dim.

YERUSHALA'IM SHEL ZAHAV
Original Hebrew Words by NAOMI SHEMER

AVIR HARIM TZALUL KAYA'IN
VERE'ACH ORANIM
NISA BERU'ACH HA'ARBA'IM
IM KOL PA'AMONIM

UVTARDEMAT ILAN VA'EVEN
SHVUYA BACHALOMA
HA'IR ASHER BADAD YOSHEVET
UVELIBA CHOMA

EICHA YAVSHU BOROT HAMA'IM
KIKAR HASHUK REIKA
VE'EIN POKED ET HAR HABA'IT
BA'IR HA'ATIKA

UVAM'AROT ASHER BASELA
MEYALELOT RUCHOT
VE'EIN YORED EL YAM HAMELACH
BEDERECH YERICHO

ACH BEVO'I HAYOM LASHIR LACH
VELACH LIKSHOR KTARIM
KATONTI MITZE'IR BANA'ICH
UME'ACHRON HAMSHORERIM

KI SHMECH TZOREV ET HASFATA'IM
KINESHIKAT SARAF
IM ESHKACHECH YERUSHALA'IM
ASHER KULA ZAHAV

YERUSHALA'IM SHEL ZAHOV VESHEL NECHOSHET VESHEL OR
HALO LECHOL SHIRA'ICH ANI KINOR

MY YIDDISHE MOMME

Words by JACK YELLEN
Music by LEW POLLACK and JACK YELLEN

RAISINS AND ALMONDS
(Roshenkis Mit Mandlen)

Traditional

SABBATH PRAYER
(From the Musical "Fiddler On The Roof")

Words by SHELDON HARNICK
Music by JERRY BOCK

wives.
(May He send you hus-bands who will care for you.) May the Lord pro-tect and de-

fend you, May the Lord pre-serve you from pain;

Fa-vor them, oh Lord, with hap-pi-ness and peace, Oh, hear our Sab-bath prayer, a-

men.

men.

a tempo

a tempo

ZUM GALLI GALLI

Traditional

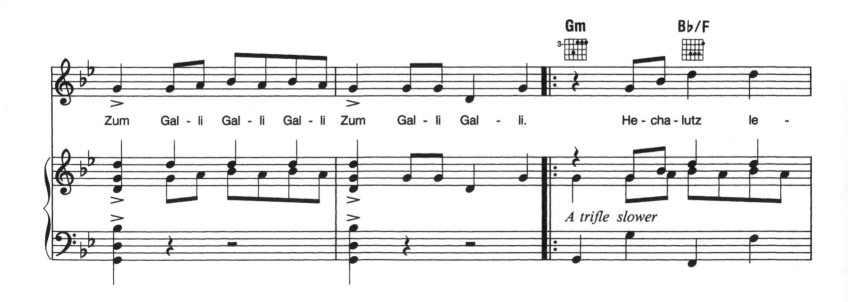

SUNRISE, SUNSET
(From the Musical "FIDDLER ON THE ROOF")

Words by SHELDON HARNICK
Music by JERRY BOCK

Moderately Slow Waltz Tempo
(soulful and wistful)